TABLE OF CONTENT

INTRODUCTION

This book was written for the quick witted thinker, individuals whom are interested in acquiring Real Estate without unnecessary jargon no one understands.

This book is also dedicated to those whom have a hard time understanding Real Estate and was discouraged.

The key to approaching the Real Estate market is to act as a Real Estate Investor opposed to an Appraiser, Agent or having been to school for Real Estate.

Having this type of mindset makes it easier to acquire, sell Real Estate and reach for you dreams in life.

Solomon Thomas-El

Chapter 1

How to acquire a Credit Card

First things first. When acting as a Real Estate Investor, it is always a good idea to get a credit card from either Lowe's or Menards (unless you have credit cards that are in good standing) or any type of Hardware Store that sells hardware goods and tools to work on properties or that deals with construction.

You must go into each establishment and speak to the manager before you fill out an application unless you have good credit and in 'good standing'.

THINGS TO DO & SAY TO MANAGER

1. You must immediately state to the manager, "I am a Real Estate Investor, and because of my dealings with selling properties I require a higher balance on a credit card offered by your establishment".

Or simply inquire to know if their establishment offers any type of line of credit for your company. The store manager will ask you a few questions like, "How are you going to pay off the credit card?"

You will stress to him/her, you sell properties and this is just a way that you can get the items you need from their establishment, which will make your job easier to sell each property.

Once the store manager hears how much you make off of each sell of a property, he should contact the office that deals with the credit cards.

You will stress to him/her that you will only purchase items from their establishment; this will make your job easier to sell each property.

At this point the manager should issue a line of credit (some cases $300) until you get your credit card in the mail, in which you will repeat this process with Meanard or any other establishment that has what you need.

CHAPTER 2

Keeping your Budget

It is always a good idea to establish a budget you can stick to in order to be successful in flipping properties.

If your budget is $80,000, you must do your homework, this will consist of pricing your labor, pricing the materials needed for repairs, pricing the Tubs, Sinks, Showers, Toilets, Cabinets, Floors, Rugs, Windows, Doors, etc.

Also things to remember are the Realtor does not get paid until the properties are sold. If you think you are about to go over on the budget, you must rethink the way you're going about flipping this house and recalculate the numbers.

When you set a budget for yourself, always add a few more dollars just in case the unexpected happens, remember you need to obtain a permit on the house, so you can work on the property in that particular location.

You can obtain this permit from a City Hall; it will cost you about $350-$400, maybe even cheaper.

ACTING AS A REAL ESTATE INVESTOR
THINGS YOU NEED TO BEGIN

1. Business Suit or Dress-Blue (earth tone colors, nothing flashy)

2. Pens and Paper or Pad

3. Calculator

4. I-Phone or smart phone

5. Business Account (something dealing with construction or real estate)

6. Flashlight, small ladder and small pitchfork

7. Magazines of the front room, Kitchens, Living Room, Bathrooms, etc. Home Improvement magazines will help you in all need to do in repairing these properties.

CHAPTER 3

How to request a R.E.O. property list from a Banker, Agent, etc.

You can go to any Bank of your choice or contact any realtor, private companies that deals with Real Estate Investors and they will be happy to give you a R.E.O. property list, requested in an intelligent tone.

You must walk into the bank, and request to speak to the manager, explain to the manager why you are there.

Tell him/her, "I am inquiring an R.E.O. Property List" (Real Estate Property Investing Listing).

Before speaking about the R.E.O. property list it's always good to do a self-interview, this interview will help to get started on your first home.

This should apply if you're new to the Real Estate Market and you "_Do Not_" have an account, if you do have an account, it should be easier to speak with your banker.

CHAPTER 4

Self-interview (sample interview)
Practice makes perfect

This is what you should say before going to the bank and preparing to speak to someone about inquiring about a R.E.O. property list. "Hi my name is_____, and I am here today to acquire an R.E.O. property list".

"I am also here to do business with your bank, as well as to make money for The Bank of (name of Bank), and for myself".

"It is my hope that we can do business here today, and if not, thank for your time". (Use this script, only if you're new to the market or do not have a business account, if you do have an account, it should be easier for you to speak to the banker, etc.)

CHAPTER 5

Location! Location! Location!

Once the Bank manager asks you what location you're interested in checking out, ask immediately for areas that are semi-high end (good areas)

Nothing in a dead zone (run down areas).

You always want properties that still have some values in them, that way when doing your walk through, all the way to the point of selling the house; it will sell without a shadow of a doubt.

CHAPTER 6

What to do upon receiving R.E.O. Property List

Once you receive the R.E.O. Property List, tell the manager that you will look over the list and let them know, you will contact them once you find the properties on the list you're interested in and the ones you think might be worth restoring.

You must remember you're a Real Estate Investor and your interest is solely to invest in Real Estate, nothing more, and nothing less.

CHAPTER 7

Properties of Value!

While looking through the R.E.O. Property list, you are looking for homes that have "*Equity in the home*" (what the house is worth via an appraiser) from the $350,000 and up.

You are also looking for the remaining balance on each home. The remaining balance should be anywhere from $5,000.00 up to $80,000.00

Once you have found five to ten of these homes, you will go back to the bank and speak to the bank manager that holds the R.E.O. Property List, let him/her know that you have found at least ten properties from the list, and you are requesting either a code number to these properties or the keys to the properties to allow you to view each property in its entirety.

As soon as a walk through is conducted you will return to the bank and you should be ready to do business with the bank.

CHAPTER 8

Walk through of the property (viewing the property)

This is for you to look through the entire property, so you will know what's needed to fix on the property, this is also where you apply *chapter 2* to the entire walk through and take notes.

A walk through consist of starting in the Basement (if there is one), the things that you are looking for in a basement are as follows:

1. A dirt basement, you do not want to purchase this property because you would have to cement the whole floor, which would cost you a lot of money and will cause you to recalculate your original budget.

2. A crack in the floor of the basement, check to see how deep the crack is. If the crack is superficial (a centimeter to 3/8 in depth). If the crack is deep and you see other cracks in the floor as deep as this one, move on to the next property (not worth fixing with so many issues with property, you're in it to flip houses with less issues).

3. Return back upstairs to the front door, look at the front door to see if it has an appealing look, if not, you will need to get a new door that will help sale this house.

At this point you will start your rough estimate on the door, you want to get a nice door that look like it cost a lot but make sure that you keep the cost of that door down as far as you can get it.

4. Walk through the front door, now you are going to start in the front room, the first thing you are looking for is "*Hardwood Floors*".

If there's carpet, pull the carpet back from each side of the four walls. You are looking for cracks in the wood, balking of the floor, or any mold.

If the floor is bad then you need to see if it is salvageable and if so you will need to check the cost for the floor to be sanded down and varnished.

5. You will need to inspect each wall in the front room and the living room; you are looking for large cracks in each wall, holes in the walls, and for termites.

You must also inspect all the wood bases, door frames, the base of the floorboards, the outlets, lights and electrical wires. Most likely you will buy all new-like outlets and wires.

The way you check the electrical wires is by standing on a ladder and pulling down one of the light fixtures to see if the wires are corroded, if you don't feel comfortable performing such task, it would be for good measures to contact an electrician.

It will cost approximately $4-5,000.00 to rewire the whole house and this is only a rough estimate, it may cost more.

6. You will do each room the same way as the way you started. The only room that need more time to investigate is the bathroom and kitchen.

All the plumbing must be checked, pipes, all fixtures on the plumbing must be replaced. Even in the basement, all major pipes must be replaced (if needed), and make sure to check for holes, rust, corrosion and mold.

7. Once you have completed the walk through of the inside of the house/property, you must turn your focus to all the windows of the house/property. You are looking for the wood to be in good shape, if not it may be wise to get all new windows.

If any windows are broken, cracked, or if there aren't any windows, you must either replace the windows or have some installed. When dealing with windows you must realize that windows are the "light of the house".

Then view the glass to see if enough sunlight comes into the house/property to tell whether you will need to replace the window.

8. The next thing that needs to be focused on is looking at the cabinets in the kitchen and the counter tops. If the cabinets cannot be salvaged, you will need to replace them with new ones.

Most of the time it is always a good idea to buy new cabinets and counter tops for a more attractive kitchen.

All the tiles and floors should be replaced with up to date appliances. Never put aluminum in the kitchen or the bathroom, this will not make the property value increase.

9. Replace all kitchen appliances like: stoves, micro-waves, refrigerators, etc. Make sure all appliances are the same color and

model. You are looking for "*State of the Art*" appliances and up to date.

10. You are now going into the bathroom to inspect the Bathtub, Shower and the Sink. If they are out dated you must replace them all.

Remember to buy fashionable products so the property value increases. If the sink, toilet, or the tub are too close to each other you will need to do the whole bathroom over to make more room for comfortability.

11. All bedrooms upstairs, hallways, should be carpeted including the stairs.

Remember to install track lights that have sensors in the hallways throughout the house/property, potential buyers will see this as a good purchase.

CHAPTER 9

The Front Yard (must be appealing)

The front yard must be appealing to the buyer; it's always a good idea to replace the grass on the property if the front of the yard is not appealing.

You should put flowers in the front yard, put trees in the front yard but do not block the windows or the door of the property.

Make sure to check the cement of the walkway of the property and the stairs of the property.

If there are cracks in the cement make sure to have them repaired, check the railing of the front porch to see if it's salvageable (only if its damaged) or need to be replaced.

CHAPTER 10

The Back Yard (must be appealing)

Before you inspect the back yard, you must inspect the garage. You are looking for holes in the garage, cracks, poor wood, or if there's concrete.

You are looking for cracks, holes in the walls, and then you should turn your focus to the roof of the garage.

You are looking for tears in the shingles, holes in the roof, or if there's a roof at all.

This will bring up the value of the property up. Remember to check the garage floor, check the concrete to see if it needs to be repaved, also check the driveway.

Now you should turn your focus back to the back yard and check the walkway that leads from the house/property to the garage.

You should next check the grass to make sure that it looks good and count how many trees are in the back yard (if any).

At this point you must focus on what would boost the property value, such as adding flowers, a tree or two, statues, or privacy fences. It's a good idea to add poles to hang laundry up and anything that will look appealing for the back yard.

The thought of adding a patio would be appealing too depending on the size of the back yard, and always look to see if you can fit a swimming pool as well (all of these add value to house/property).

CHAPTER 11

How to add up the estimate (budgeting purposes)

Now that you've went through he property you must total up a rough estimate for everything that you saw in the house that needs work on it.

At this time you will return back to bank and have your promissary note (legal document) on hand. This is what is used to buy the property and this is where you "*must*" prepare to do business with the bank without using your own money.

At this time you must contact the manager whom you previously spoken with and provide him/her with the outcome of each property.

Make sure you ask the property manager or banker if the properties are "*free and clear*" or if there are any liens, back taxes, or tree removals, street repair or any putting up of light post.

Once it is free and clear, then it is time to sit down with the manager of the bank and do business.

Here is what you will need to say to him/her, *"I hope that we can do some business today, and make money for this bank as well as for myself".*

At this time you should present the promissory note (explain the checklist), and then you should tell the manager the following: *"This is the only way that I am able to do business with you today".*

Inside the promissory note states an agreement between the bank manager or whoever is selling the properties, this agreement should have the following statement:

"The date to which I agree to pay back any money that the bank loans me, and the purchase of the properties".

It shall also tell the manager of the bank that *by accepting this promissary note, this bank is allowing me to take out an equity loan of $150,000.00 to repair the property.* The promissory note shall indicate that *the buyer of this property shall pay the bank in full within 90 days of the purchase price.*

What you are doing here is getting the property with no money of yours; you are actually getting the property with the promissory note.

Once you get the property to take out an equity loan (loan of what the property is worth) with the same bank, he/she will get a 3% to 4% interest on the loan.

Once approved for the equity loan for the property and sale, you will pay back that money you used to fix the property.

CHAPTER 12

Selling the property

In order to sell a property you must attract as many people as possible to the property. The first focus is to attract people to the property and to contact a Realtor. You should contact him/her soon as you start to fix up the property. Explain to the realtor that you are looking to sell the properties on the first day of "Open House".

Second, is the Internet, you must take pictures of every room in the house as well as the surrounding of the properties.

This way the buyer will see the whole property before they get there, this is a part of staging.

Third, you should put up flyers, signs leading to the property and use words that will help you sell the property.

CHAPTER 13

Staging the Property (setting the stage)

Staging the property can be a difficult process and fun at the same time; on the other hand if you follow the blue print of each magazine that you used to remodel the property, the idea should come to life.

The staging process should be a success; you should always add fine touches to the living room, dining room, kitchen, bathrooms, and the bedrooms.

This is a sure way that the property will sell. Always point out the special things that have been added to the property such as: the tract lights in the hallways, up and down stairs, showers, tubs, sinks, cabinets, hardwood floors, almost always the property will sell.

Also, you should add oriental rugs and floor rugs and be sure to have the electricity on and the waster turned on during this process of selling the property. It's also a good idea to have refreshments for potential buyers (finger foods, water, etc.)

CHAPTER 14

Paying back monies owed to the lender (always repay a loan)

Once the property is sold, it is your loyal duty to return your obligation of the agreement f the promissory note.

Once the checks are cut you must take the initiative to distribute out the monies to pay back the $150,000.00 (or whatever was loaned out) and to pay the credit card bill from Menards or Lowes.

After this process is completed you shall move on to the next project. You should always use the same method as if it was the first.

End Note

Please not, for starters, you must only purchase or show interest in houses/properties that are in the range of $40,000-$90,000 only, to keep overhead, interest rates down upon requesting an equity loan.

You're requesting a loan for $100,000 to $150,000, invest in the home/property the complete value of the home/property (ex. $90,000-$150,000=$60,000 overhead, upon selling the property, it must go on the market in the rage of $265,000-$285,000).

Upon property being sold at $275,000-$240,000, net profit is at $35,000 plus the $60,000 overhead, with you line of credit paid off from Menards or Lowes, you're now in good standing with all (3) companies, repeat this process enough= success in a major way.

SAMPLE PROMISSORY NOTE

Promissory Note
(Sample Promissory Note)

Allegation of Jurisdiction: State of (your state)

I,_____, on (date and moneth of year), executed and

delivered, for the location of the property at (address of property)

in which said property has an equity of $150,000.00 and up to

$450,000.00. A promissory note in the following words and

figures, whereby Mr./Mrs./Ms. (your name) has promised to pay

back the bank of_____, in full (90) days, in the

sum of $_____ for the property on (location of address).

The note will be paid in full for the above location address.

Mr./Mrs./Ms. (your name) owes the bank of (name of bank) in the

amount stated in the promissory note (amount owed). The note will

paid in full at the end of the (90) days or before the (90) days. As

this bank and Mr./Mrs./Ms. (your name) agrees to these terms of

this promissory note, it is in good faith that the agreement of

Mr./Mrs./Ms. (your name), and the bank is to be fulfilled in the amount of ($ owed) and with the banks acceptance of this promissory note, the bank of (name of bank) will allow Mr./Mrs./Ms. (your name), to take out an equity loan in the amount of (monies requesting) out of this property for repairs of this property at (location of property). It is understood there will be a percentage on the loan at a low percentage rate. This is the agreement by the Bank and Mr./Mrs./Ms. (your name) on the promissory note for the property at (location of property), it is understood that the full balance of the outstanding monies owed to the bank will be paid at the time of the property sale.

Dated:

Signed by:_____

Signed by bank of:_____

Signed by Bank Manager:_____

About the Author

SOLOMON THOMAS-EL, a Los Angeles native, author of more than five books, has written curriculum for At-Risk Youth, active member of Stillwater Writers Collective Group. Named "The next Walter Mosley and Donald Goines author of our times" by the Moorish Association for more than five years and currently lives in his home town of Watts, California.